A Special Gift

For
_____

From
_____

Date
_____

Message
_____
_____

BOUQUET OF JOY

Helen Steiner Rice

Revell
A DIVISION OF
Baker Book House Co

BOUQUET OF JOY
by Helen Steiner Rice

Originally published under the title *This Is the Day: A Daily Devotional* (calendar) by Gibson Greetings Inc.

© 1995: Christian Art, P.O. Box 1599, Vereeniging, South Africa

Designed by: Christian Art

ISBN 0-8007-7147-8

If we accept whatever God
sends as gifts of His love.
We'll be showered with
blessings from our Father above.

*I will send down showers in
season; there will be showers
of blessing.*
Ezekiel 34:26 NIV

This is the day to recite
the wise saying,
"April showers will bring
forth May flowers."

Flowers sleeping
'neath the snow,
awakening when
the spring winds blow,
Leafless trees
so bare before
are gowned in lacy green
once more.

Like the crocus, it will
burst into bloom;
it will rejoice greatly
and shout for joy.
Isaiah 35:1-2 NIV

This is the day to admire
the mystery and beauty
of nature.

Sometimes when faith
is running low
And I cannot fathom
why things are so,
I walk among the flowers I grow
And learn the answers
to all I would know.

As you have heard from the
beginning, his command is
that you walk in love.
2 John 1:6 NIV

This is the day to ponder
again what the Almighty
has done!

No one is a stranger
in God's sight,
For God is love, and in His light
May we too try in our small way
To make new friends
from day to day.

*For I was hungry and you gave
me food, I was thirsty and you
gave me drink, I was a stranger
and you welcomed me."*

Matthew 25:34-35

This is the day to reach out
to others with an open mind,
an open heart and a warm
handshake.

Keep us gently humble
in the greatness
of Thy love,
So someday
we are fit to dwell
with Thee in peace above.

And he said to the woman,
"Your faith has saved you;
go in peace."
Luke 7:50

This is the day to maintain
an unassuming attitude.
Remain humble, but
elevate someone else's
self-esteem.

Like a soaring eagle
you too can rise above
The storms of life around you
on the wings of prayer and love.

Therefore I tell you, whatever
you ask in prayer, believe
that you have received it,
and it will be yours.
Mark 11:24

This is the day to take refuge
in the shelter of God's arms.

Give us strength and courage
to be honorable and true,
Practicing Your precepts
in everything we do.

*Finally, brethren, whatever is
true, whatever is honorable,
whatever is just, whatever is
pure, whatever is lovely,
whatever is gracious, if there is
any excellence, if there is
anything worthy of praise, think
about these things.*

Philippians 4:8

This is the day to exercise and
firm you your principles.
Practice makes perfect.

Meet God in the morning and
go with Him through the day
And thank Him for His guidance
each evening when you pray.

*O Lord, my God, I call for
help by day; I cry out in the
night before thee.
Let my prayer come before
thee, incline thy ear to my cry!*

Psalm 88:1-2

This is the day to rendezvous
with God for breakfast.
Enjoy your lunch together
and take Him to dinner as
your companion.

So little do we realize
that the glory and the power
Of Him who made the universe
lie hidden in a flower.

*Worthy art thou, our Lord and
God, to receive glory and honor
and power for thou didst create
all things, and by thy will they
existed and were created.*

Revelation 4:11

This is the day to analyze a
flower, not from a botanical
perspective, but a spiritual one.
No microscope is necessary,
for with your eyes and heart you
can see the miracle, the marvel
and the power of our Creator.

Rejoice though your heart
is broken in two,
God seeks to bring forth
a rich harvest in you.

*While the earth remains,
seedtime and harvest,
cold and heat, summer and
winter, day and night,
shall not cease.*

Genesis 8:22

This is the day to expect a
bountiful yield from the seeds
of faith which you have planted
and encouraged to grow.

A mother's love
is fashioned
after God's enduring love,
It is endless and unfailing
like the love of Him above.

Serve one another in love.
Galatians 5:13 NIV

This is the day to fill
your home with love
and laughter.

We all have cares and
problems we cannot solve alone,
But if we go to God in prayer,
we are never on our own.

*He answered their prayers,
because they trusted in him.*
1 Chronicles 5:20 NIV

This is the day to enlist
the help of God.
He will listen and respond.

W e all have cares and
problems we cannot solve along,
But if we go to God in prayer,
we are never on our own.

*He answered their prayers,
because they trusted in him.*
1 Chronicles 5:20 NIV

T his is the day to enlist
the help the God.
He will listen and respond.

It's not the things that can
be bought that are life's
richest treasure,
It's just the little heart gifts
that money cannot measure.

Give, and it will be given to you.
A good measure, pressed
down, shaken together and
running over, will be poured
into your lap.
For with the measure you use,
it will be measured to you.
Luke 6:38 NIV

Avoid a materialistic outlook.
The real treasures of life
come from God.

They served
and fought and died
so that we might
be safe and free –
Grant them, O Lord,
eternal peace
and give them Thy victory!

*The Lord looks down from
heaven, he sees all the sons
of men; from where he sits ...*

Psalm 33:13

This is the day to remember
those in the past who fought
for your present-day liberties.

Some work to do,
a goal to win,
A hidden longing deep within
That spurs us on to bigger things
And helps us meet
what each day brings.

*Let us run with perseverance the
race that is set before us.*
Hebrews 12:1

This is the day to maintain
our values.
Honesty and integrity and
perseverance can never
be purchased.
They are developed within
and require constant practice.

Whenever I am troubled
and lost in deep despair,
I bundle all my troubles up
and go to God in prayer.

He said to his disciples,
"Why are you so afraid?
Do you still have no faith?"
Mark 4:40 NIV

This is the day to abide
in stillness and gain peace
of mind.

Friendship, like flowers,
blooms ever more fair
When carefully tended by
dear friends who care.

*Their life shall be like a watered
garden, and they shall languish
no more.*

Jeremiah 31:12

This is the day to recognize
Jesus as your dearest friend
and the capable caretaker
of life's garden.

When we cut ourselves away
from guidance that's divine,
Our lives will be as fruitless
as the branch without the vine.

I am the true vine, and my
Father is the vinedresser.
Every branch of mine that bears
no fruit, he takes away, and
every branch that does bear
fruit he prunes, that it may
bear more fruit.
John 15:1-2

This is the day to
nourish your life.
Some pruning is necessary,
but never allow yourself
to be cut away from the vine.

The good, green earth
beneath our feet,
The air we breathe,
the food we eat –
All these things and many more
Are things we should
be thankful for.

As the rain
and the snow come down from
heaven, and do not return to it
without watering the earth and
making it bud and flourish ...
Isaiah 55:9-11 NIV

This is the day to focus on your
blessings – visible and invisible.
Make manifest your
appreciation.

He was crucifield and buried,
but today the whole
world knows
The Resurrection story
of how Jesus Christ arose.

There they found the Eleven
and those with them, assembled
together and saying,
"It is true! The Lord has risen
and has appeared to Simon."
Luke 24:33-34 NIV

This is the day to ponder
the promise that appeared
preposterous but has been
proven possible through
Jesus Christ.

God, give us wider vision
to see and understand
That both the sun and showers
are gifts from Thy great hand.

*So if you faithfully obey the
commands I am giving you
today – to the love the Lord
your God and to serve him
with all your heart and with all
your soul – then I will send rain
on your land in its season …
so that you may gather in your
grain, new wine and oil.*

Deuteronomy 11:13-14 NIV

This is the day to cultivate
the qualities that will please
the master Gardener.

Our Father in heaven
always knows what is best,
And if you trust in His wisdom,
your life will be blessed.

*And we know that in all things
God works for the good of those
who love him, who have been
called according to his purpose.*

This is the day to confide in
God and remain confident
that He who has helped you
before will do so again.

Everyone has problems
in this restless world of care,
Everyone grows weary
with the cross they have to bear.

*And he said to all, "If any man
would come after me, let him
deny himself and take up his
cross daily and follow me."*

Luke 9:23

This is the day to develop
a sensitivity to the pain
felt by others.
Display genuine concern
and furnish assistance in
shouldering their crosses.

Thank God for good things
He has already done,
And be grateful to Him
for the battles you've won.

*For the battle is not
yours, but God's.*
2 Chronicles 20:15 NIV

This is the day to analyze
the good and the bad events
you've experienced.
The "good" list far
exceeds the bad.

When you're disillusioned,
and every hope is blighted,
Recall the promises of God,
and your faith will be relighted.

Never be lacking in zeal,
but keep your spiritual
fervor, serving the Lord.
Be joyful in hope, patient in
affliction, faithful in prayer.
Romans 12:11-12 NIV

This is the day to illuminate
your devotion to your
Creator, and your zeal
will also shine.

God never plows
in the soul of man
Without intention
and purpose and plan.

*It is the hard-working farmer
who ought to have the first
share of the crops.*
2 Timothy 2:6

This is the day to enrich
the lives of those near you.
Explain the significance
of bread and wine
and gifts originating from
the earth as wheat and grapes.

No day is too dark
and no burden too great
For God in His love
to penetrate.

*This God – his way is
perfect; the promise of the
Lord proves true;
he is a shield for all those
who take refuge in him.*

Psalm 18:30

This is the day to feel
how fortunate you are.
God loves you.

Why am I impatient
and continually vexed
And often bewildered,
disturbed and perplexed?

Amazed and perplexed,
they asked me another,
"What does this mean?"
Acts 2:12 NIV

This is the day to be
gentle and considerate.
Avoid sarcastic expressions.

Flowers sleep
beneath the ground,
But when they hear
spring's waking sound,
They push themselves
through layers of clay
To reach the sunlight
of God's day.

... the hour is coming, and now
is, when the dead will hear the
voice of the Son of God,
and those who hear will live.
John 5:25

This is the day to wake up
with a sunny smile.
Challenge yourself to
make someone happy.

A mother's love is like
a beacon burning bright
with faith and prayer,
And through the changing
scenes of life we can find
a haven there.

*Honor your father and your
mother, that your days may be
long in the land which the Lord
your God gives you.*

Exodus 20:12

This is the day to telephone
or visit your mother.
If she has passed away,
call on her by prayer.
It's your turn to become
a haven.

God's grace is
more than sufficient,
His mercy is
boundless and deep,
And His infinite blessings
are countless,
and all this
we're given to keep.

*Ask and it will be given to
you; seek and you will find;
knock and the door will be
opened to you.*
Matthew 7:7 NIV

This is the day to enumerate
your many blessings.
Thank God for His generosity.

He who was born
to be crucified
Arose from the grave
to be glorified,
And the birds in the trees
and the flowers of spring
All join in proclaiming
this heavenly King.

*... so that as Christ was raised
from the dead by the glory of
the Father, we too might walk
in newness of life.*

Romans 6:4

This is the day to glorify
the heavenly King.
Pay tribute to His Son
and praise the Holy Spirit.

God speaks to us
in many ways,
Altering our lives,
our plans and days,
And His blessings come
in many guises
That He alone in love devises.

*The Lord bless you and keep
you; the Lord make his face
shine upon you and be gracious
to you; the Lord turn his face
toward you and give you peace.*
Numbers 6:24-26 NIV

This is the day to turn the
television off and converse
with your family.
Participate in some board games.

Through dark hours
of tribulation
God gives us time
for meditation,
And nothing can be counted loss
That teaches us
to bear our cross!

In this you greatly rejoice,
though now for a little while
you may have had to suffer grief
in all kinds of trials.
1 Peter 1:6 NIV

This is the day to visualize
Christ carrying His cross, and
yours will not seem heavy.

A mother's love is something
that no one can explain –
It is made of deep devotion
and of sacrifice and pain.

*Her children rise up and call
her blessed; her husband also,
and he praises her.*

Proverbs 31:28

This is the day to practice
your spelling.
"Love" can be spelled
with only three letters –
M-O-M.

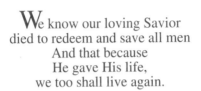

We know our loving Savior
died to redeem and save all men
And that because
He gave His life,
we too shall live again.

I tell you the truth, he who
believes has everlasting life.
I am the bread of life.
John 6:47-48 NIV

This is the day to rejoice.
Because of Christ's triumph
and resurrection we have the
promise of eternal life.

Know that the promises
of God
will never fail or falter,
And you will inherit
everlasting life
which even death
cannot alter.

*Keep your life free from love
of money, and be content with
what you have; for he has said,
"I will never fail you nor
forsake you."*

Hebrews 13:5

This is the day to renew
your spiritual fervor.
Yahweh's love will last forever

Let me be great
in the eyes of the Lord,
For that is the richest,
most priceless reward.

*The man who plants and the
man who waters have one
purpose, and each will be
rewarded according to
his own labor.*
1 Corinthians 3:8 NIV

This is the day to be
enthusiastic about the
success of others.
Better still, help others
to succeed.

When God sends sorrow
or some dreaded affliction,
Be assured that it comes
with His kind benediction.

*I will turn their mourning
into joy, I will comfort them,
and give them gladness
for sorrow.*
Jeremiah 31:13

This is the day to embrace
the sorrows of the present as
conditioners that will train you
to face the challenges
of tomorrow.

Anything and everything
can somehow be endured
If Your presence is beside me
and lovingly assured!

*Now faith is the assurance
of things hoped for,
the conviction of things
not seen.
For by it the men of old
received divine approval.*
Hebrews 11:1-2

This is the day to bestow praise
on a co-worker who deserves it.
When someone earns your
respect, let it be known.
Everyone enjoys assurance.

Let us plan
with prayerful care
to always allocate
A certain portion of each day
to be still and meditate.

I will meditate on all your
works and consider all your
mighty deeds.
Psalm 77:12 NIV

This is the day to appropriate
time and thought to
your Creator.
In quiet surroundings,
and hushed reverie thank
God for your blessings.

Love is unselfish,
understanding and kind,
For it sees with the heart
and not with the mind!

*He who does not love does not
know God; for God is love.*
1 John 4:8

This is the day to think your
comments through before
speaking, so that when you are
through speaking, you will
not have spoken all that
you thought!

The waking earth at springtime
reminds us it is true
That nothing really ever dies
that is not born anew.

*You have been born anew,
not of perishable seed but of
imperishable, through the living
and abiding word of God;
for "All flesh is like grass and
all its glory like the flower
of grass."*
1 Peter 1:23

This is the day to stir to
action the new you.

If everybody brightened
up the spot
on which they're standing
By being more considerate
and a little less demanding,
This dark old world
would very soon
eclipse the evening star –
If everybody brightened up
the corner where they are!

*You are my lamp, O Lord;
the Lord turns my darkness
into light.*

2 Samuel 22:29 NIV

This is the day to let your
own little light shine.

To know life is unending
and God's love is endless too
Makes our daily tasks
and burdens so much easier to do.

*For the wages of sin is death,
but the free gift of God is eternal
life in Christ Jesus our Lord.*
Romans 6:23

This is the day to define your
life's purpose and goal
as you contemplate God's
unconditional and endless
love for you.

Spring is God's way
of speaking to men
And saying, "Through Me
you will live again."

*For to this end Christ died
and lived again, that he might
be Lord both of the dead and
of the living.*
Romans 14:9

This is the day to scrutinize
your home before you
start spring cleaning.
If Jesus came for a visit,
would He be pleased with
what He saw and heard: your
books, magazines, videos,
conversations?

The road will grow
much smoother
and much easier to face,
So do not be disheartened –
this is just a resting place.

*My people will live in peaceful
dwelling places,
in secure homes, in undisturbed
places of rest.*
Isaiah 32:18 NIV

This is the day to avoid detours.
Your destination is heaven,
but all journeys include
some rest stops.

Spare me all trouble and save
me from sorrow –
May each happy day bring a
brighter tomorrow.

Look at the birds of the air:
they neither sow nor reap nor
gather into barns, and yet your
heavenly Father feeds them.
Are you not of more value
than they?
Matthew 6:26

This is the day to worry not.
God will take care of you.

In this world of trouble,
with darkness all around,
Take my hand and lead me
until I stand on higher ground.

*When Jesus spoke again to
the people, he said,
"I am the light of the world.
Whoever follows me will never
walk in darkness, but will have
the light of life."*
John 8:12 NIV

This is the day,
with God's assistance, to throw
a life preserver to a
sinking soul. Life preservers
are: understanding, compassion,
charity, mercy.

Life is a mixture
of sunshine and rain,
Laughter and teardrops,
pleasure and pain,
Low tides and high tides,
mountains and plains,
Triumphs, defeats and
losses and gains.

*For every matter has its time
and way, although man's
trouble lies heavy upon him.*
Ecclesiastes 8:6

This is the day to study the rose.
A rose is beautiful, but it does
have thorns which can hurt.
Life is like a rose.
Mixtures prevail everywhere.

When God makes a promise,
it remains forever true,
For everything God promises,
He unalterably will do.

*And this is what he promised
us – even eternal life.*
1 John 2:25 NIV

This is the day
to keep the promises that
you've made – to God, to
friends and to yourself.

Although I cannot
find Your hand
To lead me on to the
promised land,
I still believe with all my being
Your hand is there
beyond my seeing!

*I, the Lord, have called
you in righteousness;
I will take hold of your hand.*
Isaiah 42:6 NIV

This is the day to scrutinize
your surroundings.
If you can't locate God's
hand, be assured that He
will find yours.

I am perplexed and often vexed,
And sometimes I cry
and sadly sigh,
But do not think,
dear Father above,
I question You or
Your unchanging love.

Have mercy on me, O God,
according to your unfailing
love; according to your great
compassion blot out my
transgressions.
Psalm 51:1 NIV

This is the day to dry your tears.
Remain confident that God
loves you always, in all ways
and at all times.

Just as great nature
sends the spring
To give new birth
to each sleeping thing,
May God grant rebirth
to man's slumbering soul
And help him forsake
his selfish goal.

*Do nothing from selfishness or
conceit, but in humility count
others better than yourselves.*

Philippians 2:3

This is the day to be generous.
Share your time with someone.
Listen, really listen to a friend.
Give your undivided attention.
Refrain from interrupting.

Open your heart's door
and let Christ come in,
And He will give you new
life and free you from sin,
And there is no joy
that can ever compare
With the joy of knowing
you're in God's care.

*I am the door; if any one enters
by me, he will be saved, and will
go in and out and find pasture.*
John 10:9

This is the day to welcome
your visitor.
Christ is asking to come in.
He will bring you peace.
Don't lock Him out.

Let our prayer continue
through a joyous, waking spring
In thanking God for everything
a newborn spring can bring.

*Then many will give thanks
on our behalf for the gracious
favor granted us in answer to
the prayers of many.*
2 Corinthians 1:11 NIV

This is the day to celebrate!
You don't need a reason or an
excuse, but spring is in the air
and new life appears
everywhere.

On this Memorial Day
we offer up a prayer –
May the people of all nations
be united in Thy care.

*Blessed is the nation whose
God is the Lord, the people
he chose for his inheritance.*
Psalm 32:12 NIV

This is the day to appreciate
your freedom to speak and to
worship as you choose.

After winter comes the spring
To breathe new life
in everything,
And all the flowers
that fell in death
Will be awakened by
spring's breath.

*Therefore it is said,
"Awake, O sleeper,
and arise from the dead, and
Christ shall give you light."*
Ephesians 5:14

This is the day to perform
an act of magic.
Give a flower to an
unhappy individual.
Watch the transformation.

I am faith and I am light,
And in me there shall be
no night.

*God is light; in him there
is no darkness at all.*
1 John 1:5 NIV

This is the day to turn on the
light in someone's life.

God, grant me courage
and hope for every day,
Faith to guide me along my way,
Understanding and wisdom too,
And grace to accept what life
gives me to do.

*Be strong, and let your
heart take courage, all you
who wait for the Lord!*
Psalm 31:24

This is the day to cherish the
serenity that can be yours
when you accept the
challenges of life.

God has many messengers
we fail to recognize,
But He sends them
when we need them,
for His ways
are wondrous wise!

*Do not neglect to show
hospitality to strangers,
for thereby some have
entertained angels unawares.*
Hebrews 13:2

This is the day to study the
actions of a salesclerk, a teacher
or a bus driver. If you really
look, you can often recognize
wondrous, tenderhearted ways.

One thing never changes,
it remains the same forever –
God truly loves His children,
and He will forsake them never!

*Be strong and of good courage,
do not fear or be in dread of
them: for it is the Lord your God
who goes with you; he will not
fail you or forsake you.*

Deuteronomy 31:6

This is the day to repeat to
yourself, "God will never
abandon me, and I must
never abandon Him."

Our future will seem brighter and we'll meet with less resistance
If we call upon our Father and seek divine assistance.

Surely there is a future and your hope will not be cut off.
Proverbs 23:18

This is the day to allot a very special spot for God in your present and future schedule.
He is the source of your hope.

When your heart is heavy
and your day is dull with care,
Instead of trying to escape,
why not withdraw in prayer?

*Cast all your anxiety on him
because he cares for you.*
2 Peter 5:7 NIV

This is the day to relax a
little and pray a lot.

With nothing but sameness
how dull life would be,
For only life's challenge
can set the soul free,
And it takes a mixture
of both bitter and sweet
To season our lives
and make them complete.

*Blessed be the name of God for
ever and ever, to whom belong
wisdom and might. He changes
times and seasons.*

Daniel 2:20-21

This is the day to realize that
seasons, like gourmet
seasonings, add to the
spice and variety of life.

God, make us conscious
that Your love comes
in many ways,
And not always just as
happiness and bright and
shining days.

*I will come and proclaim your
mighty acts, O Sovereign Lord;
I will proclaim your
righteousness, yours alone.*
Psalm 71:16 NIV

This is the day to be aware that
troubles act as the polish that
keeps your faith well shined.

You can't pluck a rose
all fragrant with dew
Without part of its fragrance
remaining with you.

Cast your bread upon the
waters, for you will find it
after many days.
Ecclesiastes 11:1

This is the day to volunteer
your time for a worthy project,
and you'll enjoy the aroma
that comes from the flower
known as "giving of oneself."

Somehow the good Lord
gives us
the power to understand
That He
who holds tomorrow
is the One
who holds our hand.

*If I take the wings of the
morning and dwell in the
uttermost parts of the sea,
even there thy hand shall lead
me, and thy right hand shall
hold me.*

Psalm 139:9-10

This is the day to put your
hand into the hand of the Lord.

There is nothing that is new
beneath God's timeless sun,
And present, past and future
are all molded into one.

What has been will be again,
what has been done will be
done again; there is nothing
new under the sun.
Ecclesiastes 1:9 NIV

This is the day to know
that through the ages
and stages of life
God has always been present
and will continue to be.

The restless, unknown
longing of my searching
soul won't cease
Until God comes in glory
and my soul at last finds peace.

*Peace I leave with you; my
peace I give to you; not as the
world gives do I give to you.
Let not your hearts be troubled,
neither let them be afraid.*

John 14:27

This is the day to accept the
gift of peace presented to you
by Jesus, Son of God.

Life is a highway
on which the years go by –
Sometimes the road is level,
sometimes the hills are high.

I lift up my eyes to the hills –
where does my help come from?
My helps comes from the Lord,
the Maker of heaven and earth.
Psalm 121:1-2 NIV

This is the day to realize
that life is a highway and the
manner in which it is traveled
is up to the person behind
the wheel.

We know not how it happened
that in an hour of need
Somebody out of nowhere
proved to be a friend indeed.

Let brotherly love continue.
Hebrews 13:1

This is the day to prove you
are a friend to someone by
your word or action.

Who can see
the dawn break through
without a glimpse
of heaven and You?
For who but God
could make the day
and softly put the night away?

For salvation is nearer to
us now than when we first
believed; the night is far gone,
the day is at hand.
Romans 13:11-12

This is the day to to greet God
in the morning and bid Him
sweet dreams at night.

Keep looking for an angel
and keep listening to hear,
For on life's busy, crowded
streets you will find
God's presence near.

*Thou hast made known to
me the ways of life;
thou wilt make me full of
gladness with thy presence.*
Acts 2:28

This is the day to develop
the ability to look for
and find God in others.

God, renew our spirits
and make us more aware
That our future is dependent
on sacrifice and prayer.

*And all these blessings shall
come upon you and overtake
you, if you obey the voice of
the Lord your God.*

Deuteronomy 28:2

This is the day to revive
your soul by singing an
old, familiar hymn.
Hymns are a special form
of prayer.

When someone
does a kindness,
it always seems to me
That's the way God
up in heaven
would like us all to be.

He has showed you,
O man, what is good;
and what does the Lord
require of you but to do justice,
and to love kindness, and to
walk humbly with your God?
Micah 6:8

This is the day to walk
humbly with God by serving,
in some capacity, the least

There's but one place to go,
and that is to God, and,
dropping all pretense and pride,
We can pour out our problems
without restraint and gain
strength with the Lord at
our side.

For I, the Lord your God,
hold your right hand;
it is I who say to you,
"Fear not, I will help you."
Isaiah 41:13

This is the day to visit
with God.
The fastest way of reaching
Him is not by running,
but by kneeling in prayer.

I know He stilled the tempest
and calmed the angry sea,
And I humbly ask if in His love
He'll do the same for me.

*And he awoke and rebuked the
wind, and said to the sea,
"Peace! Be still!"
And the wind ceased,
and there was a great calm.*
Mark 4:39

This is the day to calm
the fears within.
Ask God to provide a respite
for you as He stills the
existing turmoils.

Fathers are wonderful people,
too little understood
And we do not
sing their praises
as often as we should.

Listen, my son, to your
father's instruction
and do not forsake your
mother's teaching.
Proverbs 1:8 NIV

This is the day to praise your
father and to spend some time
together either in thought,
prayer or an activity such as
fishing or going to a
baseball game.

Rest and relax and grow
stronger, let go and let
God share your load,
Your work is not finished or
ended, you've just come to a
bend in the road.

*Trust in the Lord with all
your heart, and do not rely
on your own insight.
In all your ways acknowledge
him, and he will make
straight your paths.*
Proverbs 3:5-6

This is the day to make
time for resting and relaxing.
God wants you to "float awhile"
and regain your strength.

Where there is love
there is a smile
To make all things
seem more worthwhile.
Where there is love
there's a quiet peace.
A tranquil place
where turmoils cease.

So faith, hope, love abide,
these three; but the greatest
of these is love.
1 Corinthians 13:13

This is the day to
demonstrate love.
A person can give without
loving, but never love
without giving.

The unexpected kindness
from an unexpected place,
A hand outstretched in
friendship, a smile on
someone's face,
A word of understanding
spoken in an hour of trial
Are unexpected miracles that
make life more worthwhile.

*Share with God's people who
are in need. Practice hospitality.*
Romans 12:13 NIV

This is the day to verify
that the sign on your door
says "Welcome."
Let your facial expression
say it too.

The earth is where
we live today,
and we must serve God here,
For He watches us
from way up there,
and His love
is always near.

*… even as the Son of
man came not to be served but
to serve, and to give his life as
a ransom for many.*
Matthew 20:26-28

This is the day to act in such a
manner that God will be pleased
as He watches from above.

Each time you do a kindness,
God smiles and blesses you,
For in serving those around us,
we serve and please Him too.

*A kind man benefits himself,
but a cruel man brings
trouble on himself.*
Proverbs 11:17 NIV

This is the day to
encourage a younger person.
Consider becoming a mentor.

I come to meet You, God,
as I linger here.
I seem to feel You very near –
A rustling leaf, a rolling slope
speak to my heart
of endless hope.

*From the fig tree its lesson: as
soon as its branch becomes
tender and puts forth its leaves,
you know that summer is near.
So also, when you see these
things taking place, you know
that he is near, at the very gates.*
Mark 13:28-29

This is the day to schedule
an out-of-doors conference
with God.

A̲ll we are or hope to be
Is empty pride and vanity –
If love is not a part of all,
The greatest man is very small!

You shall love your neighbor
as yourself.
Matthew 22:39

T̲his is the day to
demonstrate true humility.

You can't light a candle
to show others the way
Without feeling the warmth
of that bright little ray.

A generous man will prosper;
he who refreshes others will
himself be refreshed.
Proverbs 11:25 NIV

This is the day to speak an
unexpected word of praise.
You'll feel and see the glow
generated by that one
verbal candle.

In trouble and in gladness
we can always hear Your voice
If we listen in the silence
and find a reason to rejoice.

*Then you shall call, and the
Lord will answer; you will cry,
and he will say, Here I am.*
Isaiah 58:9

This is the day to enjoy the
quiet of a sunrise.
Look and listen!

Lord, show me the way
I can somehow repay
The blessings You've
given to me …
Lord, teach me to do
what You most want me to
And to be what You
want me to be.

*How can I repay the Lord for
all his goodness to me?
… I will fulfill my vows to
the Lord.*

Psalm 116:12, 14 NIV

This is the day to live your life
in such a fashion that others
can look for and find Christ in
you and your actions.

Seldom do we realize
the importance of small deeds
Or to what degree of greatness
unnoticed kindness leads.

*He who withholds kindness
from a friend forsakes the fear
of the Almighty.*
Job 6:14

This is the day to teach
someone a craft that you
know: baking, collecting,
crocheting, knitting, painting.

Love is unselfish,
giving more than it takes,
And no matter what happens,
love never forsakes.

*As I was with Moses,
so I will be with you;
I will never leave you
nor forsake you.*
Joshua 1:5 NIV

This is the day to see
both sides of an issue.
Try to understand the other
person's point of view.